New Horizons
in English

4

Third Edition

Michael Walker

Addison-Wesley Publishing Company
Reading, Massachusetts • Menlo Park, California • New York
Don Mills, Ontario • Wokingham, England • Amsterdam • Bonn
Singapore • Sydney • Tokyo • Madrid • San Juan

A Publication of the World Language Division

Director of Product Development: Judith Bittinger
Project Director: Elinor Chamas
Editorial: Kathleen Sands Boehmer
Manufacturing/Production: James W. Gibbons
Text Design: John F. Kelly
Cover Design: Don Taka
Illustrations: Marcy Ramsey, Walter Fournier, Akihito Shirakawa, Randy Verougstraete
Art Direction: Publishers' Graphics

Photo Credits: p. 1, © P. J. Griffiths/Magnum Photos, Inc.; p. 6, Ford Motor Co.; p. 7, Mercedes-Benz of North America, Inc., Woburn Foreign Motors, Ford Motor Co.; p. 9, Ringling Brothers and Barnum & Bailey Circus World; p. 13, © Ulrike Welsch/Photo Researchers, Inc.; p. 21, Philippe Gontier; p. 25, Focus Stock Photos, © PLI; p. 30, Ringling Brothers and Barnum & Bailey Clown College; p. 33, Jack Bailey's Studio; p. 35, Photography by Danny Lyon © 1970 Magnum Photos; p. 37 Focus Stock Photos, © PLI; p. 45, Philippe Gontier; p. 47, Ira Kirchenbaum, Stock Boston; p. 49, Focus Stock Photos, © Rubin Schlaht; p. 57, British Tourist Authority; p. 58, Camerapix/Photo Researchers, Inc.; p. 59, Interior Department/Sport Fisheries & Wildlife; p. 61, © George Holton/Photo Researchers, Inc.; p. 66, Sears, Roebuck and Co.; p. 69, W. Gibbons; p. 71, General Electric; p. 73, © Britton-Logan/Photo Researchers, Inc.; p. 81, Almqvist & Wiksell Läromedel AB; p. 85, © De Sazo/Photo Researchers, Inc.; p. 93, Addison-Wesley Archives; p. 97, © Peter Menzel/Stock, Boston; p. 105, Addison-Wesley Archives; p. 107, NASA; p. 117, © Paul Fusco/Magnum Photos, Inc.

Acknowledgements: p. 32, "The Little Girl and the Wolf" copyright 1940 James Thurber, copyright 1968 Helen Thurber from *Fables for Our Time* published by Harper and Row and from *Vintage Thurber* published by Hamish Hamilton Limited; p. 20, "Afternoon on a Hill" from *Collected Poems*, Harper and Row, copyright 1917, 1928, 1945, 1955 by Edna St. Vincent Millay and Norma Millay Ellis. Reprinted by permission of Norma Millay Ellis; p. 66, From *The Complete Poems of D. H. Lawrence* collected and edited by Vivian de Sola Pinto and F. Warren Roberts. Copyright 1964, 1971 by Angelo Ravagli and C. M. Weekley, Executors of the Estate of Frieda Lawrence Ravagli. Reprinted by permission of the publisher, Viking Penguin, a division of Penguin Books USA Inc. and Lawrence Pollinger, Ltd., London.

ISBN: 0-201-53512-2
   3 4 5 6 7 8 9 10-VH-99 98 97 96 95 94

Introduction

NEW HORIZONS IN ENGLISH is a communication-based, six-level, basal series planned and written to make the learning of English as a second language effective and rewarding. Stimulating opportunities to practice listening, speaking, reading, and writing skills develop independence and confidence in the use of English. Thoughtfully chosen vocabulary gives students the words they need to communicate in their new language in a variety of situations; carefully paced introduction of grammatical and structural concepts helps insure a strong foundation of communication skills.

Important to every learner is a sense of achievement, a feeling that he or she has successfully accomplished the tasks presented. Motivation, the desire to learn, is equally important. NEW HORIZONS IN ENGLISH is written to satisfy both needs: to provoke, through selection of topics, vocabulary, and illustrations, a genuine interest in learning more, and to pace and schedule material in such a way that achievement and mastery are facilitated.

The language used in NEW HORIZONS IN ENGLISH is contemporary and relevant. Most important, it is English that students can and will use outside the classroom. Natural exchanges and dialogues arise from the real-life situations that form unit themes. New to this edition is the addition of literature, with selections that will increase students' enjoyment of the language. Also, students will be challenged by the "Fast Track" pages in which new and varied material is presented.

The emphasis on speaking and listening, with meaning always paramount, means that oral communicative competence develops early and is broadened and deepened as students move through the series. Parallel development of reading and writing skills promotes competence in other communication areas at the same time.

Dialogues and readings from the texts, and many of the exercises, are recorded on the optional tape cassette program, which provides models of American pronunciation and intonation.

A complete program to build communicative competence, NEW HORIZONS IN ENGLISH provides motivation, mastery, and a sense of achievement. Every student—and every teacher—needs the feeling of pride in a job well done. NEW HORIZONS IN ENGLISH, with its unbeatable formula for classroom success, insures that this need will be filled.

Contents

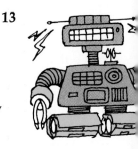

Partner Practice

There's something wrong with the **mirror.**

We'll go to the service station and get it fixed.

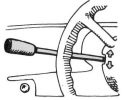

1. turn signal

2. headlight

3. battery

4. door handle

5. steering wheel

6. wiper

—Slow down! You're driving too fast.
—I'm only doing fifty.
—But the speed limit's thirty here.
—Don't worry. There aren't any police around.
—Watch out for that pedestrian!
—Hey, who's driving? Me or you?
—You are, but . . . .
—Stop acting like a backseat driver.
   We'll be at the service station in no time!

—John's **sports car** is very **fast**.
—Is it as **fast** as Bill's?
—Oh, yes. It's even **faster**.
—Really? I thought Bill's was the **fastest** one made.

 What can you say about John's other vehicles?

1. car

2. compact

3. motorcycle

4. scooter

5. station wagon

6. van

MEMORY BANK

fast	faster	fastest	expensive	more expensive	most expensive
safe	safer	safest	powerful	more powerful	most powerful
roomy	roomier	roomiest	economical	more economical	most economical
good	better	best	reliable	more reliable	most reliable
bad	worse	worst	comfortable	more comfortable	most comfortable

Mr. Mendes is at a car dealer's to look at a new car. He likes his old car, but the salesman tries his best to sell him a newer one.

MR. MENDES	THE SALESMAN
—Is this car good?	—It's the best one we have.
—But is it fast?	—It's the fastest one we have.
—Is it safe?	—It's the safest one we have.
—Is it roomy?	—It's the roomiest one we have.
—Is it comfortable?	—It's the most comfortable one we have.
—And is it popular?	—It's the most popular one we have.
—And is it reliable?	—It's the most reliable one we have.
—Is it powerful?	—It's the most powerful one we have.
—Is it economical?	—It's the most economical one we have.
—And I suppose it's expensive.	—It's the most expensive one we have.
—My old car is the cheapest one I've ever owned. I'll keep it.	

 Sell this car to a friend.

Practice making sentences with the words below.

A $\left\{\begin{array}{l}\text{taxi}\\\text{bus}\\\text{compact}\end{array}\right.$ takes $\left\{\begin{array}{l}\text{more}\\\text{less}\\\text{fewer}\end{array}\right.$ $\left\{\begin{array}{l}\text{passengers}\\\text{gas}\\\text{baggage}\end{array}\right.$ than a . . . .

A $\left\{\begin{array}{l}\text{scooter}\\\text{sports car}\\\text{van}\end{array}\right.$ doesn't take $\left\{\begin{array}{l}\text{as much}\\\text{as many}\end{array}\right.$ $\left\{\begin{array}{l}\text{gas}\\\text{passengers as a . . . .}\\\text{baggage}\end{array}\right.$

1. park   2. turn   3. pass   4. enter

Read & Understand

HENRY FORD

One day in 1893 the people of Detroit, Michigan were very surprised to see a car coming down the street. The driver's name was Henry Ford.

Henry was interested in mechanical things as a young boy. At school he was not a good student. His father wanted 5 him to be a farmer, but Henry wanted to make cars.

In 1903 he founded the Ford Motor Company. His idea was to make cars that were lighter, cheaper, and faster. His most successful car was the Model T. Ford sold fifteen million between 1908 and 1925. By 1924 the 10 factory was producing 7,500 cars each day. Ford's cars were cheap because he had his own factories for most things he needed. He even built his own ships and planes.

Ford paid his workers good money. All of them got at least five dollars a day, which was a lot in those days. 15

1. Why were the people of Detroit very surprised?
2. What do you know about Ford's father?
3. What were Ford's plans for cars?
4. In what way was the Model T successful?
5. Why were Ford's cars cheap?

ON YOUR OWN

Do you own a car? Why did you buy it? Do you like it, or not? Why? What kind of car do you want to own? Why?

Mixed Bag

1. 1991 Mercedes-Benz
   Price: $47,000
   Maximum speed: 130 miles per hour
   0 to 60 miles per hour: 14 seconds
   Gasoline mileage: 18 miles per gallon

2. 1991 Jaguar
   Price: $60,000
   Maximum speed: 135 miles per hour
   0 to 60 miles per hour: 7.2 seconds
   Gasoline mileage: 13 miles per gallon

3. 1991 Ford Festiva
   Price: $8,000
   Maximum speed: 93 miles per hour
   0 to 60 miles per hour: 11 seconds
   Gasoline mileage: 37 miles per gallon

1. Which is the most expensive car?
2. Which is the cheapest car?
3. Which is the fastest car?
4. Which is the slowest car?
5. Which car travels farthest on one tank of gas?
6. Which car travels the shortest distance on one tank of gas?
7. Which car accelerates best?
8. Do you want to own one of these cars? Why?

The Farmer and the Stork

Finding that cranes were destroying his newly—
sown corn, a farmer set a net in his field to catch the
destructive birds one evening. When he went to
examine the net the next morning he found a number
of cranes in its meshes, and a stork as well.

"Release me, I beseech you," cried the stork, "for I
have eaten none of your corn, nor have I done you
any harm. I am a poor innocent stork, as you may
see—a most dutiful bird. I honor my father and
mother. I . . ."

But the farmer cut him short.

"All this may be true, I dare say, but I have caught
you with those who were destroying my crops, and
you must suffer with the company in which you are
found."

What is the moral of this fable?

Picture This!

Who?   What?   Where?   When?   Why?

Use your imagination as you talk about the photo. Then write about the picture on your own.

Fast Track: *Read and Find Out*

Think about these questions as you read the article.

1. On a sunny day, would you need a jacket at the top or the bottom of a high mountain?
2. Vegetation means:
   a) animal life
   b) plant life
   c) the sun's energy

WHY DOES IT GET COLDER AS YOU CLIMB A MOUNTAIN?

As you climb a high mountain the air gets thinner and colder. You may think you are getting nearer the sun, but a kilometer is nothing when the sun is 150 million kilometers away! In fact, the sun heats the Earth, and it is the Earth that heats the air.

The sun's energy that reaches the Earth's surface and heats it up arrives as shortwave radiation. This is easily absorbed by the air. There is more air to absorb this heat near the Earth's surface than higher up. So the higher you go, the colder it gets.

This has an effect on the vegetation that will grow at different altitudes in mountain areas.

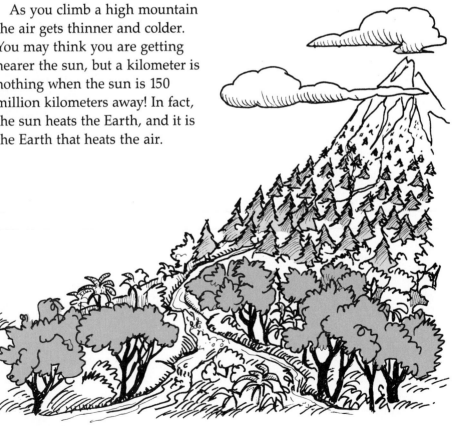

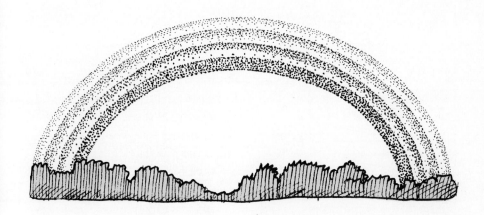

Think about these questions as you read the article.

1. Another word for *refraction* is:
   a) bending
   b) mixture
   c) arc
2. True or false:
   A rainbow can only appear in the sky above you.
3. Light rays travel:
   a) in circles
   b) in a straight line
   c) at a low angle

WHY DO WE SEE RAINBOWS?

When sunlight passes through raindrops it is slightly bent. Sunlight is a mixture of colors. The raindrops bend some colors more than others, so they are separated out to make the colors of the rainbow.

Light rays travel in a straight line, but they do change direction when they pass through sub-stances of different density, for example, from air to water. Have you ever noticed that if you look down at a drinking straw in a glass of water it appears bent? This bending is called refraction. Raindrops refract sunlight.

Sunlight has to pass through raindrops at a low angle for the colors to show as a semicircle arc. This is why you see rainbows most often after showers in the early morning or late evening, and not at midday. From an aircraft or a mountain top you can some-times see a rainbow below you as complete circle.

Listen & Understand

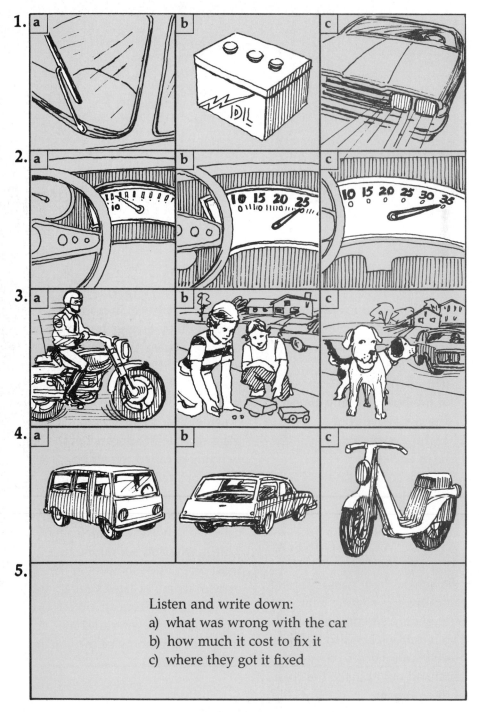

5.

Listen and write down:
a) what was wrong with the car
b) how much it cost to fix it
c) where they got it fixed

Partner Practice

Are these mice quick learners?

Oh, yes. They learn very quickly.

Is the professor intelligent?

Yes, very.

And does he learn quickly?

Oh, yes. Every time I ring this bell, he brings me food!

 Mice are intelligent, but they're not as intelligent as horses. What can you say about these animals?

1. cow/chimp

2. dolphin/shark

3. ant/worm

4. horse/rabbit

THE PROFESSOR AND HIS ROBOT

Professor Player is very proud of his latest invention, a robot. He loves to tell people how good his robot is. A reporter from the Daily News is interviewing the professor.

THE REPORTER	PROFESSOR PLAYER
—I've never heard of such a robot. Is he good at everything?	—Oh, yes. He does everything well.
—They say he's a marvelous tennis player.	—That's right. He plays tennis marvelously.
—And that he is a magnificent singer.	—True. He sings magnificently.
—And a beautiful painter.	—Correct. He paints beautifully.
—I hear that he is an elegant dancer.	—Yes, he dances elegantly.
—I guess he's a very quick learner.	—Of course. He learns very quickly.
—They say he is a superb chess player.	—That's right. He plays superbly.
—But how come your robot is so good at everything?	—Well, he has such a wonderful father, you know!

—How did you know he was impatient?
—Oh, he spoke very impatiently.

1. How did you know they were patient?
2. How did you know she was impolite?
3. How did you know he was polite?
4. How did you know they were pleasant?
5. How did you know he was unpleasant?
6. How did you know I was unhappy?
7. How did you know they were happy?

—Why did he behave so angrily?
—Because he was angry, I suppose.

1. Why did she sing so happily?
2. Why did he speak so sadly?
3. Why did they behave so nervously?
4. Why did she work so calmly?
5. Why did he drive so carelessly?
6. Why did they wait so patiently?

What did these people do? Why?

1.

2.

3.

Use the words below to talk with a friend about things you both do.

	go to the movies	
	play tennis	once a year?
	travel	once a day?
Do you	visit your grandparents	every day?
	go shopping	now and then?
	go swimming	every week?
	speak English	

			seldom
	ever	No, I	hardly ever
	usually		never
Do you	sometimes ...?		sometimes ....
	frequently		frequently
	always	Yes, I	always
	often		often

Now ask a friend if s(he):

Do you travel frequently?

1. travels frequently.
2. goes to the movies now and then.
3. goes shopping every week.
4. plays tennis every day.
5. always studies hard.
6. ever exercises.
7. usually eats fish for breakfast.
8. sometimes drives carelessly.

ON YOUR OWN

Work with a friend, and make up questions and answers of your own. Take notes about what your friend says, and be ready to tell the class about what s(he) does and how often s(he) does it.

Read & Understand

INVADERS FROM MARS

In 1938 there was a play called "The War of the Worlds" on the radio. The play started with a news report about an explosion on Mars. There was another report about a burning object falling over a farm in New Jersey.

At the same time the play began, America's most   5
popular radio show was ending on another station. Many listeners missed the very beginning of "The War of the Worlds." When they changed stations, they did not know that it was just a play.

A reporter described the object. He said it was very   10
bright and hard to look at. Suddenly a door opened. There was a scream, and the reporter was dead. Six thousand soldiers attacked the object, but only 120 lived to tell about it.

Of the six million or so people who heard the play, more   15
than two million thought it was a true news report. People telephoned the radio station for news. Thousands left their homes to escape the invaders from Mars. It was many days before life was back to normal.

How did the play end? Nobody could stop the invaders   20
except a little germ which was harmless to people from Earth, but deadly to the invaders from Mars.

1. How did the play start?
2. Why did many people miss the beginning?
3. How did the reporter describe the object?
4. What happened to the soldiers who attacked the object?
5. What stopped the invaders from Mars?

Mixed Bag

Pretend some Martians really landed on Earth. What did they think of Earth people and their customs? What did they tell their friends about what they saw on Earth? Can you guess from these descriptions what they saw?

1. An Earth person had a piece of paper with something inside it. He put it in a hole in his head. Then he set fire to it!

2. They were sitting in front of a box. At first, there was nothing. Then there was a lot of light, and noise came out of the box! None of the Earth people moved. I thought they were dead. But then the light and noise stopped, and they all got up again.

3. She put her finger in some holes in a black object. With her other hand, she put something next to her ear. Then she talked to herself for a few minutes! What a strange way to behave!

4. I saw a game I think they play. Earth persons stood outside a building. A bell rang, and they went in. Later a bell rang, and they all came out. The bell rang again a few minutes later, and they went back in. They did this all day!

ON YOUR OWN
Pretend you're a visitor from Mars. Describe some things you've seen on Earth. You can write your descriptions, too.

Afternoon on a Hill

I will be the gladdest thing
    Under the sun!
I will touch a hundred flowers
    And not pick one.

I will look at cliffs and clouds
    With quiet eyes,
Watch the wind bow down
  the grass.
    And the grass rise.

And when lights begin to
  show
    Up from the town,
I will mark which must be
  mine,
    And then start down!

Edna St. Vincent Millay

Picture This!

Who?   What?   Where?   When?   Why?

Use your imagination as you talk about the photo. Then write about the picture on your own.

Fast Track: *Read and Find Out*

Think about these questions as you read the article.

1. True or false:
   Water makes up nearly two-thirds of a person's weight.
2. Name four chemical elements found in the human body.
3. What is the most interesting fact in this article?

WHAT IS YOUR BODY MADE OF?

Your body contains over 20 different chemical elements. The most plentiful element in the body is oxygen. Oxygen, together with hydrogen, forms water. Water makes up nearly two-thirds of your weight.

The body of an average person contains about 45 liters of water. It also has an amount of carbon equal to nearly 13 kilograms of coal. Much of this carbon, together with hydrogen and oxygen, makes up fats and sugars. Carbon, hydrogen, oxygen and nitrogen form the body's vital proteins.

There are also large amounts of calcium and phosphorus. The body contains over one and a quarter kilograms of calcium and enough phosphorous to make over 2,000 matches. The body also contains a couple of spoonfuls of sulphur, enough iron to make a 2.5 centimeter nail, and nearly 30 grams of other metals.

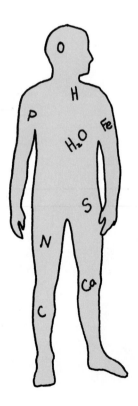

Think about these questions as you read the article.

1. What are germs?
2. True or false:
   All viruses cause disease.
3. Make a chart showing the three
   types of germs and examples of
   the diseases they cause.

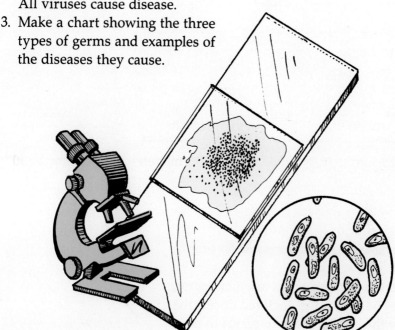

WHAT ARE GERMS?

A germ is a tiny living organism that causes disease.

The world's smallest living organisms include bacteria and viruses and tiny single-celled animals, or protozoa. Some of these are harmless or even useful. Others cause disease and are sometimes known as germs.

Most protozoa are harmless, but a few, such as the malaria parasite and the dysentery amoeba, are disease-causing organisms.

Harmful bacteria may cause disease themselves or they may produce poisonous waste substances. Bacterial diseases include most kinds of food poisoning, bubonic plague, diptheria, pneumonia, scarlet fever, typhoid fever, typhus and whooping cough.

There are vast numbers of different viruses. Most cause disease. Colds, chicken pox, influenza, measles, mumps and poliomyelitis are all caused by viruses. Some types of cancer are thought to be caused by virus infection.

Pronunciation

I.

popular	wrong	stop	economical
rocks	drop	dioxide	dolphin
closet	hot	job	lost

II.

most	only	don't	colder
volcano	own	soldier	robot
explosion	hole	molten	low

III. *Try these tongue-twisters just for fun!*

When a doctor doctors another doctor,
does he doctor the doctored doctor the
way the doctored doctor wants to be
doctored, or does he doctor the doctored
doctor the way the doctoring doctor
wants to doctor the doctor?

Oliver Oglethorpe ogled an owl and an oyster.
Did Oliver Oglethorpe ogle an owl and an
oyster?
If Oliver Oglethorpe ogled an owl and an
oyster,
Where's the owl and oyster Oliver Oglethorpe
ogled?

3

Do you like my new coat?
Yes, you look marvelous in it.
TOKYO
WORLD TOUR
MITSUBISHI ELECTRIC
京セラ
ショウルーム

Partner Practice

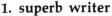

She's a **great actress.**

Yes, and what a **great film** this is!

1. superb writer   novel
2. brilliant performer   performance
3. wonderful singer   song
4. fantastic entertainer   show
5. marvelous guitarist   concert

Isn't this **great acting?**

Yes, what **great acting!**

1. superb writing
2. brilliant performing
3. wonderful singing
4. fantastic entertainment
5. marvelous music

She makes great films.

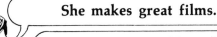

Yes, what great films she makes!

1. He writes superb novels.
2. He gives brilliant performances.
3. She sings wonderful songs.
4. He gives fantastic shows.
5. She gives marvelous concerts.

What can you say about these people?

1.   2.   3.

—What's for lunch?
—**Chicken.**
—It smells **good.**
—Thanks. I hope it tastes as **good** as it smells.

1. delicious

2. terrific

3. wonderful

4. awful

5. bad

6. terrible

—Do you like my new **dress?**
—Yes, it's **wonderful.**
—Do you really think so?
—Yes, and you look **wonderful** in it.

1. elegant

2. marvelous

3. pretty

—What do you think of this **record?**
—It's **marvelous.**
—Do you really like it?
—Yes, it sounds just **marvelous.**

1. beautiful

2. superb

3. fantastic

—How did you know he was **freezing?**
—He started to turn **blue!**

1. angry   red
2. scared   pale
3. seasick   green
4. shocked   white
5. embarrassed pink

—Why didn't you wait for me last night?
—I *did* wait. But then I became **impatient,**
 so I left.

1. nervous   2. angry
3. bored   4. worried
5. upset   6. tired

—**It's cold this winter, isn't it?**
—**Yes, the winters are getting colder.**

1. It's warm this spring, isn't it?
2. It's dry this fall, isn't it?
3. It's mild this evening, isn't it?
4. It's stormy this winter, isn't it?
5. It's cloudy this morning, isn't it?
6. It's rainy this weekend, isn't it?

—What kind of **an actor** is he?
—A **terrible** one.
—How does he **act?**
—**Terribly,** of course!

1. a conductor	brilliant	conduct	brilliantly
2. a painter	wonderful	paint	wonderfully
3. a dancer	superb	dance	superbly
4. a singer	pleasant	sing	pleasantly
5. a writer	poor	write	poorly
6. a speaker	bad	speak	badly

Simon is a brilliant conductor, but he plays badly. What can you say about these people?

1. Mary

2. Ted

3. Anna

Read & Understand

CLOWN COLLEGE

Did you know that you have to go to college to become a clown? That's right. If you want to work under the Big Top as a clown for the Ringling Brothers and Barnum & Bailey Circus, you must successfully complete the stringent course of studies at the Clown College in Venice, Florida. It is a highly competitive school. Several thousand applicants fill out lengthy application forms and only a few dozen people are selected.

The College is located in a big concrete tent. There is a big sign on the side of the tent that says "The Greatest Show on Earth!" This building is where the circus stays each winter and where it prepares the show that goes on the road each spring.

The Clown College began in 1967 when Ringling Brothers changed owners. At that time there were only 14 clowns in the circus. Today, there are over 50 clowns, almost all of them graduated from Clown College.

Going to Clown College is like going to boot camp in the army. Students have to work 14 hour days, six days a week. Clowns work hard. They have to be well-conditioned athletes and they work year round. They love their work and they love their audiences!

Mixed Bag

MEETING A STAR

    On Saturday morning at 9:30, I was walking down High Street, looking for a record store. A man stopped me and asked me the way to the Ritz Hotel. I wasn't sure exactly where it was, but I walked with him to the end of
5 High Street. He was very friendly, and his face looked so familiar. Then I remembered where the Ritz was and told him how to get there. He thanked me and tried to give me something. I thought it was money. I said 'no' at first, but he really wanted me to have it, so I took it.

10   I found the record store and listened to a few records. The "Fantastic Five" had a new record that was number two in the top twenty. I decided to buy it. I looked in my bag for my wallet and found a piece of paper the man gave me. It was a photo. I was so surprised! He was a singer
15 in the "Fantastic Five!"

Now write your own story. Here are some questions to help you if you find it difficult.

ON YOUR OWN
1. Where were you?
2. What were you doing?
3. What was the time?
4. Who stopped you?
5. What did s(he) want?
6. What was s(he) like?
7. Where did s(he) want to go?
8. How did you help him/her?
9. Did s(he) give you anything?
10. How did you find out who s(he) was?

The Little Girl and the Wolf *by James Thurber*

One afternoon a big wolf waited in a dark forest for a little girl to come along carrying a basket of food to her grandmother. Finally a little girl did come along and she was carrying a basket of food. "Are you carrying that basket to your grandmother?" asked the wolf. The little girl said yes, she was. So the wolf asked her where her grandmother lived and the little girl told him and he disappeared into the wood.

When the little girl opened the door of her grandmother's house she saw that there was somebody in bed with a nightcap and nightgown on. She had approached no nearer than twenty-five feet from the bed when she saw that it was not her grandmother but the wolf, for even in a nightcap a wolf does not look any more like your grandmother than the Metro-Goldwyn lion looks like your teacher. So the little girl took an automatic out of her basket and shot the wolf dead.

What is the moral of this fable?

Picture This!

Who?   What?   Where?   When?   Why?

Use your imagination as you talk about the photo. Then write about the picture on your own.

Fast Track: *Read and Find Out*

Think about these questions as you read the article.

1. True or false:
   A blow on the "funny bone" makes you laugh.
2. Where is the ulnar nerve located?
3. How is the ulnar nerve different from most nerves in the body?

WHAT IS YOUR "FUNNY BONE"?

Your "funny bone" is a place on the elbow where a nerve passes close to the surface. A sharp knock stimulates this nerve and the brain registers pain.

There is nothing funny about being struck on the "funny bone." This part of the elbow may have been given its name because people thought that it had something to do with the humerus, the bone of the upper arm. But, in fact, the humerus is not involved at all. The "funny bone" is the knob on the back of the ulna of the forearm.

Most nerves lie well-protected in layers of muscle. However, the ulnar nerve, which runs from the hand to the spinal cord, passes over the elbow just underneath the skin. If it is struck sharply, a stream of impulses is sent to the spinal cord and the brain registers a sharp pain in the elbow. The effect may also be felt as tingling in the fingers.

Think about these questions as you read the article.

1. True or false:
   People would feel better if they didn't sweat.
2. Describe two ways the body loses heat.
3. Sweating occurs through a process of _____.

WHY DO WE SWEAT?

Sweating is a vital process for cooling you down when you get too hot. Sweat is produced by the sweat glands on the surface of the skin. There it evaporates and cools the body.

Your body prefers to operate at its normal temperature. So when your body temperature gets too high, such as during strenuous exercise, you need to lose heat. There are two ways in which this happens.

First, the tiny blood vessels in your skin increase in size and fill with blood, giving you a flushed appearance. Heat travels from the blood to the outside air.

When your body becomes even hotter, your sweat glands produce a mixture of water and waste chemicals known as sweat. When water evaporates, it uses up a great deal of heat. So as the water in your sweat evaporates from your skin, it takes heat rapidly from your body.

Listen & Understand

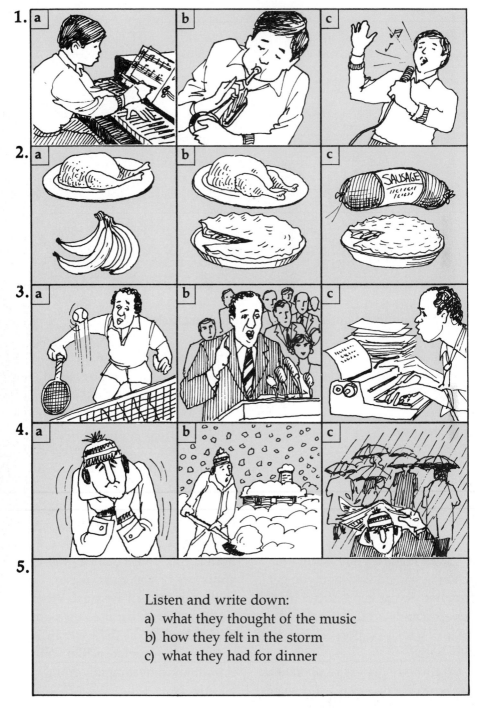

5.

Listen and write down:
a) what they thought of the music
b) how they felt in the storm
c) what they had for dinner

Partner Practice

—Somebody's **at the door**.
—I don't hear anybody.
—Well, go see.
—No, nobody's there.

1. in the hall   **2. in the kitchen**   **3. behind the curtains**

—I thought I saw something **in the yard**.
—I didn't see anything.
—Well, look again.
—There's nothing there.

1.   **2.**   **3.**

—Do we have any **cookies**?
—Let me look.
—There were some yesterday.
—No, sorry. There are none left.

1.   **2.**   **3.**

—Is this Tom's 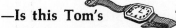 ?
—Yes, he forgot to take it with him.

1. Is this Mary's ?

      2. Is this your mother's ?

3. Is this your father's ?

      4. Is this your parents' ?

Be careful!
5. Is this my ?

      6. Is this your ?

 The Webster family is going on vacation.
Mr. Webster is helping with the packing.

Do the children need their raincoats?

Yes, remind them to take their raincoats with them.

1. Do the boys need their bathing suits?
2. Does Mary need her camera?
3. Does John need his knife?
4. Do you and Peter need your boots?
5. Do you need your glasses?

—Who made **your breakfast?**
—I made it myself.

1. **Tom's lunch**
2. **the girls' dinner**
3. **Nancy's dress**
4. **your bookcase**
5. **your and Jane's beds**

—What's the matter with **you?**
—I just made a fool of **myself.**

1. **Susan**
2. **your father**
3. **those boys**
4. **you and Jack**

—Did **you** have a good time last night?
—Yes, I enjoyed **myself** immensely.
—How **do you** feel now?
—Not so good.

1. **John**
2. **your sister**
3. **your guests**
4. **you and your wife**
5. **you**

REMEMBER:	
myself	ourselves
yourself	yourselves
himself	themselves
herself	

—Isn't that my **book?**
—No, it isn't yours. It's **mine.**
—Are you sure?
—Yes. **I** bought it **myself.**

1. his

2. hers

3. ours

4. theirs

5. his

6. mine

—Does that **car** belong to **Tom?**
—No, it doesn't. It's not **his.**
—Whose car is it, then?
—I don't know.

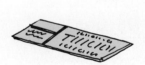

1. you

2. the Browns

3. your mother

4. Jack and Meg

5. me

6. your grandfather

Read & Understand

SOCIAL CUSTOMS AND BEHAVIOR

Social customs and ways of behaving change. Today, people can do many things that "polite" people didn't do many years ago. In the past, if a man thought of himself as a gentleman, it was impolite behavior to smoke on the street.

Customs also differ from country to country. Does a man walk on the left or the right of a woman in your country? Or doesn't it matter? What about table manners?

The important thing to remember about social customs is not to do anything that could make other people feel uncomfortable — especially if they are your guests. There is an old story about a rich gentleman who had a dinner party. When the food came, one of the guests started to eat his peas with a knife. The other guests were amused or shocked, but the gentleman calmly picked up his knife and began to eat in the same way. He didn't want to make his guest feel foolish or uncomfortable.

1. In your country, on which side of a woman does a man walk when they are on the sidewalk?
2. In the old story, what did one of the dinner guests do?
3. What did the gentleman do? Why?
4. In your country, what are two very impolite things a person could do?

Mixed Bag

WHAT DO YOU SAY?
1. You meet somebody in the morning.
2. Somebody introduces you to somebody else.
3. You step on somebody's foot.
4. You can't hear what somebody is saying.
5. You want to thank somebody who has just helped you.
6. Somebody thanks you for helping him.
7. You are leaving a very nice party.
8. Somebody has helped you carry some heavy packages.
9. You need somebody to help you push your car.
10. You meet an old friend after a long time.

WHAT'S THE WORD?
1. That's very . . . of you.
2. You two can make dinner . . . .
3. This book belongs to you—it's . . . .
4. That scarf isn't Mary's—it's not . . . .
5. We made our breakfast . . . .
6. Do you . . . if I smoke?
7. Oh, I beg your . . . .
8. I'm so sorry. It was my . . . .
9. This is my camera—it's . . . .
10. This isn't their car. That one over there is . . . .

ON YOUR OWN
Has somebody been very polite or impolite to you lately?
When? Where were you? What happened? How did you
feel? What did you do or say?

Have *you* been polite or impolite to somebody lately?
When? Where? Why? What did you do/say?

The Night Has a Thousand Eyes

The night has a thousand eyes,
    And the day but one;
Yet the light of the bright world dies
    With the dying sun.

The mind has a thousand eyes,
    And the heart but one;
Yet the light of a whole life dies
    When love is gone.

Francis William Bourdillon

Picture This!

Who?   What?   Where?   When?   Why?

Use your imagination as you talk about the photo. Then write about the picture on your own.

Fast Track: *Read and Find Out*

Think about these questions as you read the article.

1. Wind is caused by the _____ of the sun.
2. A strong wind is usually caused by a difference in:
   a. heat
   b. atmosphere
   c. pressure
3. Where do you think the strongest winds could be found—in a warm climate or a cold climate?

WHY DO WINDS BLOW?

The sun's heat warms the air and makes it move. This movement is called a wind.

Different parts of the Earth receive different amounts of heat. Near the equator, the sun is overhead and heats the Earth intensely. Nearer the poles, the sun's rays strike the Earth at a low angle so the heat is not so intense.

A lot of the Earth's heat is reflected back into space, by the atmosphere, clouds, dust in the air and by water, snow and ice. So some parts of the Earth are warm and some are cold.

Warm air tends to rise and creates areas of low pressure. Cold air tends to sink and creates areas of high pressure. As warm air rises, cold air flows in and replaces it. The greater the pressure difference, the stronger the wind blows.

Think about these questions as you read the article.

1. What is an iceberg?
2. True or false:
   The largest icebergs come from Antarctica.
3. There is a saying in English: "That's just the tip of the iceberg." What do you think that saying means?

WHAT ARE ICEBERGS?

Icebergs are huge lumps of ice which have broken away from ice sheets and glaciers and drift in the sea. When ice floats in water, only about a ninth shows above the surface. The rest is hidden beneath the water, and may damage ships.

In the northern hemisphere, icebergs come from the Greenland ice sheet. The world's tallest iceberg, 167 meters high, was sighted off western Greenland in 1958.

The largest icebergs are found in the southern hemisphere and come from Antarctica. The largest ever recorded was 335 kilometers long and 97 kilometers wide (31,000 square kilometers in area). It was measured in the South Pacific in 1956.

Icebergs may break from a glacier and fall into the sea. Usually, icebergs form from a glacier which extends into the sea. Waves, tides and floating movements of the ice cause huge pieces of ice to break off and float away.

Pronunciation

I. superb   concert   surprised   nerve

    earth   birthday   pressure   iceberg

    worst   learner   further   certain

II. speak   cheap   dream   piece

    thief   speed   cheek   heat

    sweep   briefcase   seat   keep

III. *Try these tongue-twisters just for fun!*

A right-handed fellow named Wright,
In writing, "write" always wrote "right."
    Where he meant to write right,
    If he'd written "write" right,
Wright would not have wrought rot writing "rite."

There's no need to light a night light
    On a light night like tonight;
    For a night light's a slight light
    On a light night like tonight.

Partner Practice

—Do you like this **blouse?**
—No, I don't.
—Why not?
—I don't like the **stripes.**

1. polka dots   **2. plaid**   **3. pleats**

4. checks   **5. ribbons**   **6. buttons**

—Can you help me fix this **dress?**
—What's wrong with it?
—The **hem** isn't right.

1. collar   **2. waistband**   **3. lapel**

4. cuff   **5. sleeve**   **6. zipper**

MEMORY BANK

1. dress	2. robe	3. pair of slacks
4. tie	5. hat	6. shirt
1. coat	2. skirt	3. jacket
4. raincoat	5. sweater	6. pair of jeans

—What's your **jacket** made of?
—It's made of **cotton**.

1. wool

2. silk

3. nylon

4. plastic

—What are your **shoes** made of?
—They're made of **leather**.

1. cotton   2. canvas   3. rubber   4. nylon

ON YOUR OWN

1. Work with a friend. Talk about what you're wearing right now. What is each piece of clothing made of? Then choose another person in the class to talk about.

2. What are your favorite clothes? Why? What do you wear to the movies? To a disco? To a dinner party?

Practice making sentences with the words below.

Food			grocery stores.
Furniture	is		department stores.
Medicine			drugstores.
Clothing			clothing stores.
		sold at	
Toys			toy stores.
Tools	are		hardware stores.
Books			bookstores.
Appliances			appliance stores.

—Where were these **nails** bought?
—At the **hardware store.**
—Well, take them back. They're no good.

—Where was this **meat** bought?
—At the **grocery store.**
—Well, take it back. It's no good.

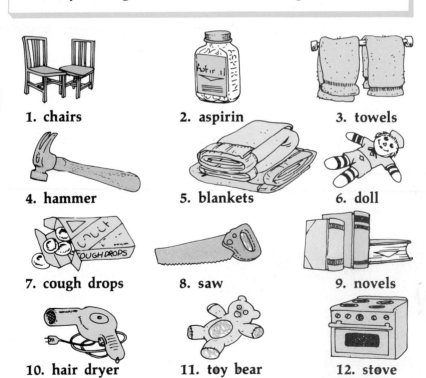

1. chairs

2. aspirin

3. towels

4. hammer

5. blankets

6. doll

7. cough drops

8. saw

9. novels

10. hair dryer

11. toy bear

12. stove

—Where can I buy **a can of hair spray?**
—It's sold at either the **supermarket**
 or the **drugstore.**

1. a tube of lipstick

2. a pack of
   cigarettes

3. a pound of
   potatoes

4. a pair of scissors

5. a gallon of paint

6. a bottle of aspirin

7. a box of nails

8. a set of tools

9. a book of
   matches

10. a loaf of bread

11. a tube of
    toothpaste

12. a pack of gum

Read & Understand

Charles of New York showed his spring collection yesterday. This year's colors for both men and women will be yellow and black. A lot of young men will be upset to hear that hair will be shorter this year.

Women will wear dresses that go right from the neck to the ankle. Waistbands are out! Cotton and nylon will be popular. Patterns will be popular, especially checks, stripes, and polka dots.

The most exciting news in men's fashions is pants which stop just below the knee! Sleeves are out, so jackets will be sleeveless. Shirts will be very daring, in bright colors with no cuffs or collars. Ties are out — scarves are in.

Charles just announced today that the president has ordered his first pair of knee-length pants!

Mixed Bag

Describe what women wore "around the house" in 1902. What do women wear at home today? What's your favorite at-home outfit?

The Oak and the Reed

A proud oak grew upon the bank of a stream. For a full hundred years it had withstood the buffeting of the winds, but one day there came a violent storm. The great oak fell with a mighty crash into the swollen river and was carried down toward the sea.

Later the oak tree came to rest on the shore where some reeds were growing. The tree was amazed to see the reeds standing upright.

"How ever did you manage to weather that terrible storm?" he asked. "I have stood up against many a storm, but this one was too strong for me."

"That's just it," replied the reed. "All these years you have stubbornly pitted your great strength against the wind. You were too proud to yield a little. I, on the other hand, knowing my weakness, just bend and let the wind blow over me without trying to resist it. The harder the wind blows the more I humble myself, so here I am!"

What is the moral of this fable?

Picture This!

Who?   What?   Where?   When?   Why?

Use your imagination as you talk about the photo. Then write about the picture on your own.

Fast Track: *Read and Find Out*

Think about these questions as you read the article.

1. The two kinds of elephants in the world today are the _____ and the _____ .
2. Name three ways these elephants are different from one another.
3. An elephant uses its _tusks_ as a weapon and to dig for water.

HOW MANY KINDS OF ELEPHANTS ARE THERE?

The two species of elephants in the world today are the African and the Asiatic, or Indian, elephant.

Elephants are the largest living land animals and the larger of the two species is the African elephant. It can grow to a height of about three and a half meters at the shoulder and may weigh over six tons.

The African elephant has a less prominent, more rounded forehead than the Asiatic elephant. Its ears and tusks are larger and it has a hollow back.

An elephant's trunk is really the nose and upper lip joined together. It is a long, flexible tube which the elephant uses for carrying food and water to its mouth, dust-bathing and smelling the air.

An elephant's tusks are actually overgrown incisor teeth. They are used as weapons and for digging for water in times of drought.

Think about these questions as you read the article.

1. True or false:
   Bats have very good eyesight, especially at night.
2. How does *echo-location* work?
3. One might compare the bat's ability to "see" in the dark to that of a:
   a. cat
   b. submarine
   c. insect

HOW DO BATS FIND THEIR WAY IN THE DARK?

A bat does not have good eyesight, but is able to "see" by sound waves. It produces a series of high-pitched squeaks which are reflected back by the objects around it.

The way in which bats find their way about is called echo-location. They produce high-pitched squeaks that humans cannot hear. Some bats, such as the long-eared bat, produce these sounds from their mouths. Others, such as the greater horseshoe bat, produce the sounds from their noses. The returning echoes are picked up by the bat's large, sensitive ears.

The bat receives information about the direction, loudness and pitch (high or low notes) of echoes returning from a flying insect. It can then work out the direction, distance and speed of the insect with amazing accuracy.

Listen & Understand

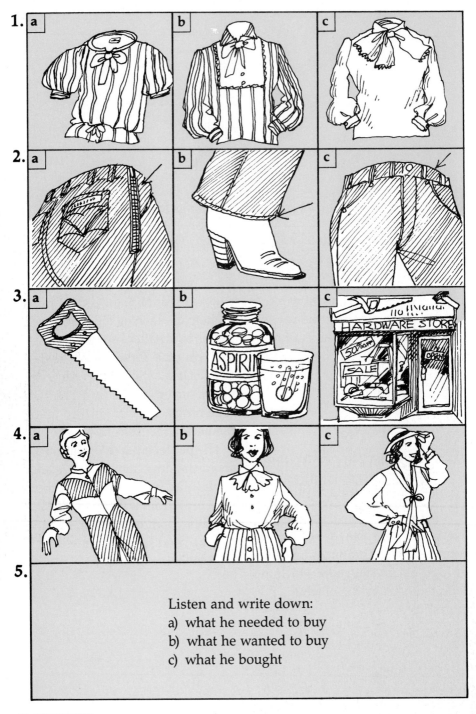

1. a   b   c

2. a   b   c

3. a   b   c

4. a   b   c

5. Listen and write down:
   a) what he needed to buy
   b) what he wanted to buy
   c) what he bought

6

Have you ordered the tickets to London?
Yes, they've already been delivered.
RIO DE JANEIRO
WORLD TOUR

Partner Practice

—How much **is that battery?**

—**$50.** You can put 10 percent down
and pay the rest on time.

—How much are the monthly payments?

—They're **10 dollars.**

Maria Rodrigo works very hard at the office. Her boss never thinks she is busy enough, however. Every morning, he asks her what she did the day before.

THE BOSS	MARIA
—Did you check the catalogues?	—Yes sir. They were checked last night.
—Did you call for the latest reports?	—Yes sir. They were called for last night.
—Did you type all the letters?	—Yes sir. They were typed last night.
—Did you pay the bills?	—Yes sir. They were paid last night.
—Did you deliver cash to our accountant?	—Yes sir. It was delivered last night.
—Did you send my baggage to the airport?	—Yes sir. It was sent last night.
—Did you order the new furniture?	—Yes sir. It was ordered last night.
—Did you sort the mail?	—Yes sir. It was sorted last night.
—Well, what have you done this morning?	—Cleaned out my desk. I quit!

> —Have you **ordered the beds?**
> —Yes, I think **they've been ordered.**

1. delivered the dryers
2. fixed the washing machines
3. paid the bill
4. sorted the mail
5. sent the packages
6. ordered the stereo

> —When will they **mail**
>   **the letter?**
> —It will be **mailed**
>   **later today.**

1. deliver the order   delivered before noon
2. print the catalogue   printed in January
3. fix the lawn mower   fixed next week
4. send the package   sent at two o'clock
5. sort the mail   sorted tomorrow
6. pay the bill   paid next month

 What are they saying?

—I'd like to buy some furniture, but I can't afford it.
—Well, **chairs** can be bought on time, you know.

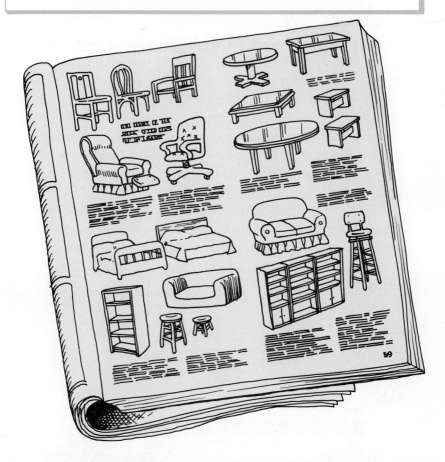

—Have they **mailed the letter** yet?   —No, but they know it must be mailed today.

1. delivered the order   delivered
2. printed the catalogue   printed
3. fixed the lawn mower   fixed
4. sent the package   sent
5. sorted the mail   sorted
6. paid the bill   paid

Read & Understand

BUYING BY MAIL

You have probably seen ads in newspapers or on TV for mail-order firms. Perhaps a catalogue has been sent to you. Why do people buy things they have not seen in person? Some people believe that things can be bought more cheaply by mail. Another advantage of buying by mail is that it is more comfortable to sit at home and look through a catalogue than to rush around the stores. With a catalogue from a large firm, you have your own store window for almost everything you want to buy.

Buying from a catalogue is so easy. It saves the shopper time and trouble. Sometimes, it saves the shopper money on one item. But people often buy more than they can really afford because most catalogues accept all the major charge cards.

Here are some items from a mail-order catalogue. Your teacher will help you understand the information you need to order the items.

(14 and 15)   Exterior-mount Mirrors
CONSTRUCTION: Adjustable, reversible heads and stainless steel mounting brackets. Non-glare glass.
INSTALLATION: Mount on either side of car. No drilling. Screw into old mirror holes.
ORDERING INFORMATION:

(14)   Mirror for Ford cars. Rectangular head, 5½x3¼ inches wide. 5⅜x3-in. mirror.
28 G 20046—Wt. 2 lbs. 3 oz. ....Each $5.79

(15)   Mirror for GM cars. Rectangular head, 5⅛x3¹¹/₁₆ inches wide. 5⅜x3-in. mirror.
28 G 20042—Wt. 2 lbs. 3 oz. ....Each $5.79

(16) Genuine Walnut wood steering Wheel
CONSTRUCTION: Hand-rubbed walnut; polished rivets, solid steel rim. Tongue and groove joints.
ORDER INFO: Requires install. kit—order below.
28 G 3202—13½x4-in. Wt. 3 lbs. 11 oz. $27.99
28 G 3203—15½x4-in. Wt. 3 lbs. 5 oz....... 29.99

Mixed Bag

Pretend you have bought some clothes from a mail-order company. The package you received in the mail did not contain what you ordered from the catalogue. Write a letter to the manager of the company. Tell him what is wrong with your order, and tell him how upset you are about the poor service. The following sentences will help you write your letter.

1. Tell him what you ordered—describe the clothes in detail.
2. Tell him when you sent the order.
3. How long did it take for the package to arrive?
4. What's wrong with the clothes? Is the color wrong? The size? The pattern?
5. Is your bill correct?
6. Do you want your money back, or a new order?
7. Will you ever shop by mail again? Why or why not?

WHAT'S THE WORD?

1. My car won't start. I think the . . . is dead.
2. I need four new . . . for my car.
3. You can see what you buy by mail in a . . . .
4. You can . . . things by mail from a mail-order firm.
5. Ten percent down is the . . . .
6. Pay the rest of the money . . . .
7. The monthly . . . are ten dollars.
8. The mail carrier delivers the mail; the secretary . . . it.
9. This bill must be . . . on time.
10. I've ordered the furniture, but it hasn't been . . . yet.

To Women, As Far as I'm Concerned

The feelings I don't have I don't have
The feelings I don't have, I won't say I have.
The feelings you say you have, you don't have.
The feelings you would like us both to have,
    we neither of us have.
The feelings people ought to have, they never have.
If people say they've got feelings, you may be pretty
  sure they haven't got them.
So if you want either of us to feel anything at all you'd
  better abandon all idea of feelings altogether.

D. H. Lawrence

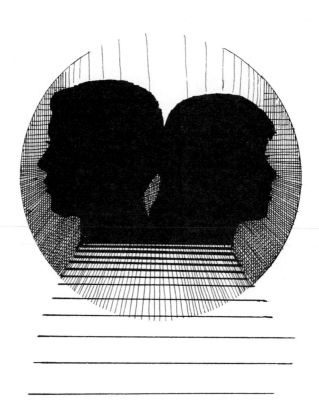

Picture This!

Who?   What?   Where?   When?   Why?

Use your imagination as you talk about the photo. Then write about
the picture on your own.

Fast Track: *Read and Find Out*

Think about these questions as you read the article.

1. Where and when did Galileo live?
2. Why is Galileo considered the first modern scientist?
3. Astronomy is the study of:
   a. the Middle Ages
   b. experiments
   c. stars and planets

WHO WAS THE FIRST MODERN SCIENTIST?

Many people consider that the first modern scientist was Galileo, who lived in Italy from 1564 to 1642. The important scientific discoveries made in ancient Greece were lost during the Dark Ages and Middle Ages. After they were rediscovered, Galileo was the first great scientist to advance science to make new discoveries.

Galileo was the first person to use a telescope in astronomy and he made several important discoveries, including the moons of Jupiter. He also found out how objects move when they fall. He did this by timing the movement of balls rolling down a slope.

By conducting experiments and using measurement to prove that his ideas were correct, Galileo laid down the principles of the experimental method that modern scientists use to make discoveries.

Think about these questions as you read the article.

1. Microwaves are like _____ waves.
2. Why does food cook quickly in a microwave oven?
3. Why do you suppose micro-wave ovens have become so popular?

HOW DOES A MICROWAVE OVEN WORK?

A microwave oven does not have burning flames or red-hot plates like gas and electric stoves. You put the food into a metal box and press a switch. Inside the box, invisible heat rays bombard the food and cook it very quickly.

A microwave oven gets its name from the rays that cook the food, which are called microwaves. They are like radio waves, and the rays heat up objects in the same way as the sun's rays warm us. However, microwaves penetrate into the food, so that it cooks on the inside as well as the outside. In any ordinary oven, it takes time for the heat to get to the inside of the food. Microwaves heat up the inside immediately, which is why a microwave oven cooks or heats up food so quickly.

Some microwave ovens contain small computers that automatically cook the food at the correct tem-perature for the right length of time.

Pronunciation

I. afraid   make   payment   able

     waist   vacation   patient   taken

     delay   nails   paper   behave

II. back seat   gallon   pattern   thank

     ads   plastic   package   maximum

     catalogue   fan   act   sat

III. *Try these tongue-twisters just for fun!*

Moses supposes his toeses are roses,
     but Moses supposes erroneously;
For nobody's toeses are posies of roses,
     As Moses supposes his toeses to be.

A flea and a fly in a flue
Were caught, so what could they do?
     Said the fly, "Let us flee."
     "Let us fly," said the flea.
So they flew through the flaw in the flue.

Partner Practice

—Call the **Police Department** right away!

—What's the emergency?

—A bad accident on Highway 2.

1. Fire Department

A fire in Gina's Restaurant

2. Ambulance Service

An injured child in the park

3. Coast Guard

A sinking boat in the harbor

4. Poison Information Center

A baby who drank gasoline

5. Red Cross

A flood

—Why don't you have a party?
—Because I don't know where to have it.

1. Why don't you park the car?
2. Why don't you buy some fruit?
3. Why doesn't he plant the tree?
4. Why doesn't she build a house?
5. Why don't they catch the bus?

—Why didn't you ask somebody for help?
—Because I didn't know who to ask.

1. Why didn't you follow somebody to the theater?
2. Why didn't she pay somebody for the tickets?
3. Why didn't he hire somebody as a driver?
4. Why didn't they thank somebody for the present?
5. Why didn't they arrest somebody for the robbery?

—Why didn't you buy anything?
—Because I didn't know what to buy.

1. Why didn't she say anything?
2. Why didn't they do anything?
3. Why didn't he order anything?
4. Why didn't she wear anything?
5. Why didn't you drink anything?

—Do you know that **doctor?**
—Yes, **she's** the one who showed me around the **hospital.**

1. firefighter   fire station

2. police officer   police station

3. nurse   medical school

4. ambulance driver   emergency room

—Do you recognize the **squad car?**
—Yes, it's the one that was parked **outside the prison.**

1. in front of the hospital

2. on the bridge

3. inside the fire station

4. in front of the hotel

—The police set up a roadblock here.
—So this is where they set up
  the roadblock.

1. The police arrested the thieves here.
2. The Fire Department had a station here.
3. The medical school had a hospital here.
4. The ambulance service had an emergency phone here.

—The police saved that old man.
—So that's who the police saved.

1. The car hit that little boy.
2. The Fire Department rewarded that girl.
3. The police protected that man.
4. The bus knocked down that pedestrian.

—There's the car that crashed
  into the wall.
—So that's what crashed
  into the wall.

1. There's the fire engine that delayed the traffic.
2. There's the car that damaged the motorcycle.
3. There's the ambulance that woke you up.
4. There's the truck that broke through the roadblock.

ON YOUR OWN

Find a story in a local newspaper or magazine about an
emergency—a fire, robbery, rescue, etc. The story can
be in English, or in your own language. Read it carefully,
and then be ready to be an "eyewitness" to the emergency.
Your classmates will ask you what you saw.

Read & Understand

EMERGENCY CALLS

You may never be part of an emergency situation, but you need to know how to get help if one does occur. The telephone book in the United States has emergency numbers on the inside front cover.

```
┌─────────────────────────────────────────────────────────────────┐
│                    EMERGENCY NUMBERS                              │
│                                                                   │
│   ┌──────────────┐  ┌──────────────┐  ┌──────────────────────┐   │
│   │     FIRE     │  │    POLICE    │  │       DOCTOR         │   │
│   │              │  │              │  │                      │   │
│   │ BOSTON   911 │  │ BOSTON   911 │  │ (Boston Emergency Physicians Service) │
│   │              │  │              │  │ BOSTON      482-5252 │   │
│   │ BROOKLINE 911│  │ BROOKLINE 911│  │ BROOKLINE            │   │
│   │              │  │              │  │ (Middlesex South District Medical Society) │
│   │ CAMBRIDGE    │  │ CAMBRIDGE    │  │ CAMBRIDGE   625-4774 │   │
│   │   876-5800   │  │   864-1212   │  │ SOMERVILLE           │   │
│   │ SOMERVILLE   │  │ SOMERVILLE   │  │ Other Places         │   │
│   │   623-1500   │  │   625-1212   │  │ (write in your number here) │
│   │ Other Places │  │ Other Places │  │                      │   │
│   │ (write in your number here) │ (write in your number here) │      │
│   └──────────────┘  └──────────────┘  └──────────────────────┘   │
│                                                                   │
│   AMBULANCE                  DOCTOR (Personal) _ _ _ _ _ _ _      │
│          (write in your number here)     (write in your doctor's number here) │
│                                                                   │
│   COAST GUARD.........223-6978   POISON..........232-2120        │
│        (Search and Rescue)           (Information Center)         │
│                                                                   │
│   F. B. I. ...............742-5533   RESCUE, Inc.......426-6600   │
│     (Federal Bureau of Investigation)  (Devoted to the prevention of suicide) │
│                                                                   │
│        ★ U. S. SECRET SERVICE        223-2728                    │
│                                                                   │
│       OR DIAL "0" - OPERATOR IN ANY EMERGENCY,                   │
│       WE ARE ALWAYS THERE AND READY TO HELP!!                    │
│       IF you cannot stay at the telephone, give the operator your │
│       city or town as well as your street and number, or the exact│
│       location where help is needed.                              │
└─────────────────────────────────────────────────────────────────┘
```

Notice that the number for the police and fire departments is the same, and that it is an easy number to remember. If you are too upset or excited to remember any numbers at all, however, you can simply dial "0" for operator in any emergency.

What number do you dial . . .

1. if you see a fire?
2. if a child drinks something poisonous?
3. if you see a boat sinking?
4. if you live in Boston and you need a doctor?
5. if somebody is trying to kill himself/herself?
6. if you have to get to the hospital quickly?
7. if you live in Somerville and you need the police?
8. What must you tell the operator if you dial "0"?

Mixed Bag

Read the following description of an accident.

At ten o'clock this morning, I was at the drugstore. I was buying a bottle of aspirin. Suddenly I heard a car. I looked out and saw a blue station wagon on South Street. It was going at least sixty miles an hour. The driver was on the wrong side of the street. The traffic lights were red, but he didn't stop. He crashed into another car. The driver of the station wagon jumped out and ran down King's Street. He was a tall, thin man with blond hair.

ON YOUR OWN

Now write a story of your own. The questions below will help you.

1. Where were you at ten o'clock?
2. What were you doing?
3. What did you hear?
4. What did you do then?
5. What did you see?
6. How fast was the car going?
7. Which side of the street was it on?
8. Were the traffic lights red or green?
9. What did the car crash into?
10. What did the driver do?
11. What did the driver look like?

The Rooster and the Ring

A farmer's wife once lost a diamond ring in the farmyard. She searched for it everywhere but as darkness fell she realized sadly that it was lost forever.

A few days later a rooster was scratching among the stones when he saw something glittering in the sunlight. He pecked at it eagerly, thinking it might be some new kind of grain, but it was so hard that it almost shattered his beak.

"Well," he said to himself, burying it deep in the earth again, "you may be a fine stone to some people, I suppose, but you are no use to me. Give me a good grain of barley any day."

What is the moral of this fable?

Picture This!

Who?   What?   When?   Where?   Why?

Use your imagination as you talk about the photo. Then write about the picture on your own.

Fast Track: *Read and Find Out*

Think about these questions as you read the article.

1. When did Christopher Columbus set sail?
2. What did he call the new people he discovered?
3. In the United States, there is a holiday called Columbus Day. Why?

WHY WERE THE FIRST AMERICANS CALLED INDIANS?

When Christopher Columbus set sail in 1492 he hoped to reach Asia and the rich Spice Islands of the Indies. Instead he found a New World and a new people, whom he called "Indians."

Columbus guessed that the Earth was round. By sailing west, he expected to reach the Indies faster than by sailing east, around Africa. He did not know that a huge continent, America, was in the way. So, when his ships reached the West Indies, he thought he must be in Asia and that the people living on the islands must be Indians. Many Indians were killed or enslaved by the Europeans who followed Columbus.

Think about these questions as you read the article.

1. The Black Death is another name for _____ .
2. Another word for <u>ravaged</u> might be:
   a. attacked
   b. enjoyed
   c. swelled
3. True or false:
   The Black Death killed about half the population of Asia and Europe.

WHEN DID THE BLACK DEATH SWEEP ACROSS THE WORLD?

The Black Death was an outbreak of bubonic plague. It ravaged Asia and Europe between 1334 and 1351.

Bubonic plague is named after the buboes, or swellings, that appear on the bodies of its victims. It has been known at least since the days of the Romans, and possibly existed in Biblical times.

The epidemic of plague known as the Black Death started in central Asia. It was carried by fleas that lived on rats. Ships and overland trading caravans carried the plague westwards. By 1346 it had reached the Crimea. From there it was carried to Europe by ships.

The plague reached Europe in 1348. By the end of 1350 it had swept through most of Europe. The outbreak was over by the end of 1351. About one person in three died from the plague during this time. Bodies were carted away for burial by corpse-collectors.

Listen & Understand

5.

Listen and write down:
a) who they called
b) why they called
c) where the emergency was

8

This neighborhood used to be so clean and quiet.
Yes, what a shame it's so dirty and noisy now.
PARIS
WORLD TOUR

Partner Practice

This **street** used to be **quiet**.

Yes, but now it's very **noisy**.

1.

2.

3.

4.

5.

MEMORY BANK

1. store	small	large
2. park	clean	dirty
3. TV	cheap	expensive
4. magazine	exciting	boring
5. chair	comfortable	uncomfortable

It's a dark, windy night in the middle of November. Two men are standing at a bus stop by a cemetery.

HENRY	GEORGE
—Hi, George. I haven't seen you for ages!	—I haven't been too well lately.
—Why don't we have lunch soon? I usually eat at the Crown Restaurant.	—I used to go there, too. But I don't have the time nowadays.
—How about a drink, then?	—Sorry. I used to drink, but I had to give it up.
—Do you have any cigarettes?	—Sorry. I used to smoke, but I had to give it up.
—How about some tennis this weekend? You used to be good.	—Sorry. I had to give it up.
—Hmmmm. You're not enjoying life like you used to, George.	—You're right. I gave it up.
—What? What do you mean?	—Poor Henry. You don't know what's happened, do you?
—I know that bus is late. I catch it right at 9.	—You mean "used to catch," Henry. You'll never ride that bus again.
—What do you mean? That bus goes right by where I live.	—You mean "used to live," Henry; you died this afternoon. You're a ghost. I'm a ghost, too!

—Have you talked about buying a new **car?**
—Yes, but we've decided not to.

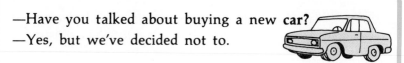

1. **2.** **3.** **4.**

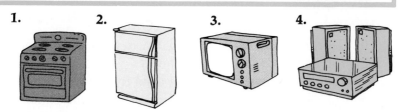

—Why did he go to the **appliance store?**
—He went there to buy a **hair dryer.**

1.

2.

3.

—You can **stop** now.
—Pardon?
—I said that you could **stop** now.

1. go   4. rest
2. open the window   5. leave
3. close the door   6. sit down

MEMORY BANK

1. hardware store	hammer	saw	box of nails
2. department store	sofa	tie	pair of shoes
3. drugstore	brush	tube of lipstick	can of hair spray

—Are you sure he'll **go by train?**
—I'm not sure, but he said he might.

1. drive   **2. take a plane**   **3. ride his bike**   **4. hitchhike**

—I can't find my **money!**
—You'd better look in your **wallet.**

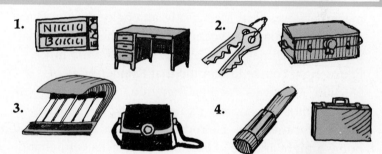

1.   **2.**

3.   **4.**

—Would you like a new **stove?**
—No, I'd rather keep my old one.

1.   **2.**   **3.**   **4.**

MEMORY BANK

1. ticket   desk   2. keys   trunk
3. matches bag   4. lipstick briefcase

1. vacuum cleaner   2. washing machine   3. sofa   4. suitcase

Read & Understand

HISTORIC FLIGHT ACROSS CHANNEL — June 12, 1979

Just after dawn, a strange flying machine with wings wider than a DC-9's took off from the beach at Folkstone, England. Just 2 hours and 49 minutes later, it landed at Cap Gris-Nez in France, 23 miles away.

The "pilot and engine," as he likes to call himself, was Bryan Allen, a 26-year-old from California. Wearing nothing more than running shorts, leather cycling shoes, a plastic crash helmet, a red life jacket, and his glasses, Allan pedaled his way over the English Channel to the $210,000 prize offered by British industrialist Henry Kremer.

The brain behind the Albatross — the name of the flying machine — was Paul MacCready, an engineer from Pasadena, California. Two years earlier, another of his pedal-powered machines, The Condor, finished a 1.15 mile-figure-eight course to win the first Kremer prize of $86,000. Allen was the pilot then, too.

The "pilot and engine" explained how he prepared himself for the flight. He rode three hours a day, slept eight hours a night and ate like a horse for weeks beforehand. On the big day, he ate bread and fruit — the best fuel — just before taking off at 5:10 a.m.

At the first attempt, a wheel broke. Mechanics quickly replaced it. The second attempt was better. Allen climbed to 20 feet and pedaled at a regular 70 revolutions per minute. "If you start sinking, you have to pedal faster," explained Allen.

Halfway over the Channel, the wind started to blow against him. His speed dropped from 12 miles per hour to only 9½. The Albatross sank to only 6 inches over the waves. Somehow, Allen pedaled fast enough to climb again to 10 feet. Finally, he saw France in front of him. It was a classic "first" in flight. The Albatross was taken to the Paris Air Show.

Mixed Bag

Below is a part of a train schedule. Study the information carefully, and then answer the questions.

NEW YORK — WASHINGTON, D.C.

	New York Penn. Sta. Leave	Philadelphia (Penn Central Sta.) Leave	Washington Arrive
167 The Night Owl (Monday-Thursday)	4:20 am	6:05	8:30 am
101 Metroliner (daily)	7:30 am	8:46	10:34 am
103 Metroliner (Mondays thru Thursdays)	8:30 am	9:48	11:34 am
173 The Minute Man (daily, except Sunday)	4:45 pm	6:16	8:23 pm
182 The Senator (daily)	7:30 pm	9:13	11:20 pm
186 Metroliner (daily)	8:30 pm	9:43	11:30 pm

ONE-WAY FARES (Double for round-trip)

Between New York and	In Metroliner Coaches	In Regular Coaches
Trenton	$12.25	$7.25
Philadelphia	17.25	11.75
Baltimore	29.00	23.50
Washington	32.00	27.00

1. What is the earliest train to Washington? What time does it arrive?
2. What time does **The Senator** stop in Philadelphia?
3. What time does **The Minute Man** leave New York?
4. Do you take the **103 Metroliner** if you want to arrive in Washington early on a Sunday morning?
5. Do you take **The Minute Man** if you want to meet a friend in Philadelphia for lunch?
6. How much is a one-way ticket between New York and Philadelphia by **Metroliner** coach? By regular coach?
7. How much is a round-trip ticket between New York and Washington by regular coach? By **Metroliner** coach?

The Tide Rises, the Tide Falls

The tide rises, the tide falls,
The twilight darkens, the curlew calls;
Along the sea-sands damp and brown
The traveller hastens toward the town,
    And the tide rises, the tide falls.

Darkness settles on roofs and walls,
But the sea, the sea in the darkness calls;
The little waves, with their soft, white hands,
Efface the footprints in the sands,
    And the tide rises, the tide falls.

The morning breaks; the steeds in their stalls
Stamp and neigh, as the hostler calls;
The day returns, but nevermore
Returns the traveller to the shore,
    And the tide rises, the tide falls.

Henry Wadsworth Longfellow

Picture This!

Who?   What?   Where?   When?   Why?

Use your imagination as you talk about the photo. Then write about the picture on your own.

Fast Track: *Read and Find Out*

Think about these questions as you read the article.

1. True or false:
   The Aborigines of Australia built towns and lived as farmers.
2. True or false:
   The early inhabitants of a place are generally treated well by new settlers.
3. Try to find out about "Aborigines" in other cultures and tell the class what you discovered.

WHERE DO ABORIGINES LIVE?

Aborigines are a country's earliest inhabitants. The best-known Aborigines are those of Australia.

Australian Aborigines have dark-brown skin and wavy hair. Their ancestors may have migrated from South-East Asia about 40,000 years ago.

Aborigines lived in small wandering bands and made simple shelters at resting places. They used weapons and tools made from wood and stone to hunt and gather food. One of their weapons was the boomerang. This is a throwing weapon made from wood. One type is clearly designed to return to the thrower.

Australian Aborigines had their own music, art and religion. At times they would gather for a corroboree, a festival of music and dancing.

There were about 300,000 Aborigines in Australia when Europeans first arrived there two hundred years ago. Many Aborigines were persecuted by European settlers, and now only about 110,000 remain.

Think about these questions as you read the article.

1. True or false:
   Eskimos are related to the people of Asia.
2. Another word for *cope* might be:
   a. fight
   b. live
   c. hunt
3. Name three ways that Eskimos
   keep warm in the winter.

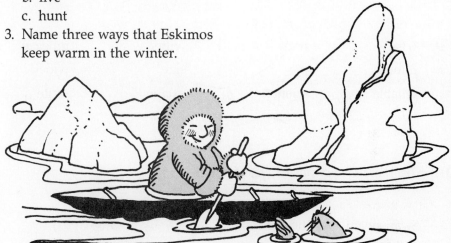

WHERE DO ESKIMOS LIVE?

Eskimos live in the cold polar regions of North America and North-East Asia. They are related to the Chinese and Japanese. Their ancestors probably migrated across the Arctic thousands of years ago.

Eskimos are well built to survive long cold, Arctic winters. Their short, stocky bodies store heat better than those of tall, thin people.

Eskimos have learned how to cope with the cold. They make warm fur coats and build turf-roofed homes, half hidden underground. In winter, hunters far out on the ice build snow houses called igloos.

Eskimos are skilled at fishing and hunting seals and whales. Their hunting boats are slim, skin-covered canoes called kayaks. On land, teams of dogs haul sleds that carry equipment and dead game. But old ways of life are dying. Many Eskimos now live in wooden houses in towns.

Pronunciation

I.

chin	hitchhike	lipstick	killer
fit	his	invaders	mechanics
quick	print	fiction	wish

II.

wise	wine	wiper	mileage
mine	pie	size	wider
reliable	science	excite	write

III. *Try these tongue-twisters just for fun!*

Swan swam over the sea —
    Swim, swan, swim;
Swan swam back again,
    Well swum, swan.

    Betty Botta bought some butter.
"But," said she, "this butter's bitter!
      If I put it in my batter,
    It will make my batter bitter.
     But a bit o' better butter
    Will but make my batter better."
So she bought a bit o' butter
    Better than the bitter butter,
    Made her bitter batter better.
     So 'twas better Betty Botta
    Bought a bit o' better butter.

Partner Practice

> Do you really want to go to **England?**

> Yes, I'm looking forward to seeing **the Houses of Parliament.**

1. the Statue of Liberty

2. St. Peter's Basilica

3. the Pyramids

4. the Eiffel Tower

5. Machu Pichu

6. Sugarloaf Mountain

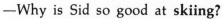

—Why is Sid so good at **skiing?**
—He's a good **skier** because he
practices **skiing** every day.

1. **skin diving**
   skin diver

2. **wrestling**
   wrestler

3. **singing**
   singer

4. **boxing**
   boxer

5. **climbing**
   climber

6. **jumping**
   jumper

—Why does Peter hate **swimming?**
—Maybe it's because he's bad
   at **swimming.**

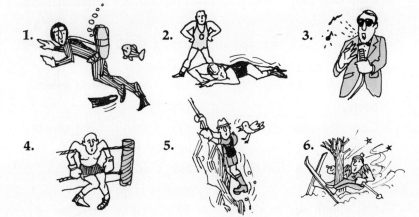

1.

2.

3.

4.

5.

6.

Fran wants to go to the races, but she has a problem. She has no way to get there, nothing to wear, and no money for the tickets! She decides to call her friend Pat.

FRAN	PAT
—Hi, Pat. Would you like to go to the races today?	—Okay. I don't mind going.
—Great! Can you lend me your blue jacket?	—Yes, I don't mind lending it to you.
—Can you drive your car?	—Yes, I don't mind driving.
—Can you pick me up?	—Yes, I don't mind picking you up.
—Can you take me home?	—Yes, I don't mind taking you home.
—Can you pick up the tickets?	—Yes, I don't mind picking up the tickets.
—Can you pay for them, too?	—No. I don't have any money.
—Oh. Then we can't go.	—That's okay with me. I don't mind not going.

—Do you **play chess** often?
—Oh, yes. I really enjoy
  playing chess.
—No. I don't enjoy **playing chess.**

1.   2.   3.

4.   5.   6.

—What do you do all day?
—**Sleep.**
—You mean you spend all your time **sleeping?**
—I most certainly do!

1.   2.   3.

4.   5.   6.

MEMORY BANK

1. play tennis	2. swim	3. sail
4. play baseball	5. dance	6. read
1. watch TV	2. jog	3. exercise
4. cook	5. eat	6. paint

HOW ABOUT YOU?

What do you enjoy doing? How often do you do it? How
do you spend your time on Saturdays and Sundays?

Read & Understand

THE GREAT TRAIN ROBBERY

At 3 a.m. on August the 8th, Jack Mills was sitting at the controls of the mail train from Glasgow to London. The train had thirteen coaches. At the end of the train, seventy-one workers were sorting the mail. Inside the second coach, there were only five workers and 128 bags full of five-pound   5
notes! The last time this train was robbed was more than 100 years ago.

At three minutes past three, Mills and his helper, David Whitby, saw a yellow warning light. They slowed the train, and then stopped. Whitby went to the telephone   10
beside the track. It was out of order. Then he saw a man creeping between the second and third coaches. Before Whitby could give a warning, he was knocked down by two men.

The robbers disconnected the last ten coaches. Then   15
they ordered Mills to drive the train to a bridge that crossed a road. At the bridge, the bags of money were unloaded from the train and thrown into trucks. One of the robbers looked at his watch at 3:45 and said, "That's enough." The robbers escaped with more than £2,500,000!   20

It was a classic "first" in big-money robberies.

1. What were the seventy-one workers at the end of the train doing?
2. Why did Jack Mills stop the train?
3. Why was it impossible to telephone for help?
4. What did the robbers do with the bags of money?
5. Why do you think they had to stop at 3:45?
6. How much is £2,500,000 in the money of your country?

Mixed Bag

On Wednesday morning at eleven o'clock, I was walking down Main Street. Suddenly I heard two shots! They came from the bank. I ran toward the bank. I saw a man coming out. He was short and chubby with red hair. He had a bag of money and a gun. He escaped in a car. That afternoon I saw the robber again at the movies! I telephoned the police. They arrived in less than five minutes and arrested the man. The bank gave me a $100 reward!

ON YOUR OWN

Now write a story of your own. The questions below will help you.

1. What day was it?
2. What time was it?
3. What did you suddenly hear?
4. Where did you run to?
5. What did you see?
6. What did the robber look like?
7. What did he have in his hands?
8. How did he escape?
9. Where did you see the robber again?
10. What did you do?
11. How much was your reward?

The Old Man and Death

An old man, stooped by age and hard work, was gathering sticks in the forest. As he hobbled painfully along he thought of his troubles and began to feel very sorry for himself.

With a hopeless gesture he threw his bundle of sticks upon the ground and groaned: "Life is too hard. I cannot bear it any longer. If only Death would come and take me!"

Even as the words were out of his mouth Death, in the form of a skeleton in a black robe, stood before him. "I heard you call me, sir," he said. "What can I do for you?"

"Please, sir," replied the old man, "could you please help me put this bundle of sticks back on my shoulder again?"

What is the moral of this fable?

Picture This!

Who?   What?   Where?   When?   Why?

Use your imagination as you talk about the photo. Then write about the picture on your own.

Fast Track: *Read and Find Out*

Think about these questions as you read the article.

1. True or false:
   The tongue is sensitive to five main kinds of taste.
2. True or false:
   Both your nose and your mouth contain special receptor cells.
3. From reading this article, try to draw a sketch showing how the receptor cells work.

HOW DO YOU TASTE AND SMELL THINGS?

Your nose and mouth contain special receptor cells. When these are stimulated by chemical molecules, they send nerve impulses to the brain.

Your tongue is covered with tiny lumps of papillae. On the sides of some papillae are small groups of cells known as taste buds. Each taste bud contains between 4 and 20 receptor cells with short sensory hairs. These react to molecules of food dissolved in your saliva.

Your tongue is sensitive to 4 main kinds of taste. Bitterness is tasted at the back of the tongue, sourness is tasted at the sides and sweetness is tasted at the front.

Saltiness is tasted all over, especially at the tip.

Your smell receptors are in the roof of the nasal (nose) cavity. They have sensory hairs that branch and project into the mucus that lines the cavity. Molecules in the air dissolve in the mucus and stimulate these hairs. There are about 15 different kinds of smell receptors, and they can detect over 10,000 different smells.

Think about these questions as you read the article.

1. True or false:
   The computer was invented in
   1896.
2. Another word for *complicated*
   might be:
   a. machine
   b. system
   c. difficult
3. Find at least four uses for a
   computer in this article. Try to
   think of more things a computer is good for.

WHAT GOOD IS A COMPUTER?

Since the first computer was
invented in the 1940s, scientists
have found countless ways to
make use of them. Large computers are used in research labora-
tories to solve complicated mathe-
matical problems. Computers in
factories help run the machinery
and keep track of materials.

In hospitals, computers help
doctors and nurses care for their
patients. Computers are vital in
planning and carrying out mis-
sions in space and under the sea.
Computers can regulate the
lighting and heating systems of
homes and offices. Computers
make it possible to publish newspapers, magazines and books
more efficiently. You might even
have a little computer in your
watch!

Listen & Understand

1. a) [map of Italy]   b) [blank map]   c) [building]

2. a)   b)   c)

3. a) ARRIVAL ....8:00   b) ARRIVAL ...7:30   c) ARRIVAL ...8:40

4. a)   b)   c)

5. Listen and write down:
    a) what Bud is good at
    b) what Jim is bad at
    c) what Pam enjoys doing

Partner Practice

What would you like to be?

I'd like to be a **pilot**.

Oh, you'd be good at that.

1. a TV announcer   **2. a reporter**   **3. a dentist**

4. a veterinarian   **5. an architect**   **6. a lawyer**

7. an engineer   **8. a mechanic**   **9. an electrician**

—My brother doesn't have any money.
—Why don't you lend him some?
—I don't have any either.

1. My father doesn't have any books.
2. My mother doesn't have any lipstick.
3. You don't have any stamps.
4. Tom and his sister don't have any blankets.
5. You don't have any tools.

—Bill doesn't have a pen, but Wendy has.
—Can't he borrow one from her?
—No. She doesn't have an extra one to lend him.

1. Harry doesn't have a tie, but Bill has.
2. Marty doesn't have a sweater, but Amy has.
3. Alice doesn't have a pen, but Hank has.
4. Mike doesn't have a pencil, but Tom has.
5. Ann doesn't have a racket, but they have.

Fill in with either *borrow* or *lend*.

1. I can't find my book. I'll have to . . . one from Tom.
2. Can you . . . me some money?
3. Why don't you . . . me money, since you just got paid?
4. Never . . . Jack anything — you'll never get it back!
5. Can I . . . your car tonight?
6. Did you . . . these books from the library?
7. Please . . . me a dollar until tomorrow.
8. I really don't like to . . . people money.
9. Did you . . . my racket to Sue?
10. Jack wants to . . . some towels from us.

—What's he doing?
—He's doing nothing at all.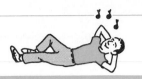

1. What's she doing?   some housework
2. What's mother doing?   the dishes
3. What's Harry doing?   his job
4. What's father doing?   business with Mr. Monk
5. What's Sheila doing?   her homework
6. What's Randy doing?   me a favor
7. What's Joe doing?   his best

—**What do rich people do?**
—**Rich people make money.**

1. What do poor students do?   many mistakes
2. What do clever people do?   good impressions
3. What do popular people do?   friends
4. What do politicians do?   speeches
5. What do judges do?   decisions
6. What do people who try   an effort
   hard do?

 Fill in with the correct forms of **do** or **make**.

1. He is very successful. He . . . a lot of business
   with Japan.
2. Tom is doing poor work in chemistry. He needs to
   . . . an effort.
3. Mary is so popular. She . . . friends all over
   the world.
4. Rock musicians . . . a lot of money.
5. Father is . . . the dishes.
6. You need to study more. You . . . too many mistakes.
7. Can you . . . me a favor?
8. I can . . . the work if you don't have time.
9. Bill always . . . a bad impression.
10. The president . . . a fine speech last week.

—He's a good talker, isn't he?
—I don't know. I can never
  make him talk.

1. He's a good singer,
   isn't he?

2. She's a good dancer,
   isn't she?

3. They're good swimmers,
   aren't they?

4. She's a good player,
   isn't she?

—Why did **you** do that?
—I didn't want to.
  Tom made **me** do it!

1. she

2. he

3. they

4. you two

Read & Understand

AN UNUSUAL PERSON

Amy Johnson was a very ambitious and energetic person. She didn't have much in common with other girls in her school, however. She played football and made a bad impression on some of her teachers. She studied at a university and later worked as a typist. But not for long — she didn't want to be a typist. She dreamed of becoming a pilot.

Amy moved to London, borrowed some money, and learned to fly. Nobody, however, wanted to hire a female pilot. She decided to fly alone to Australia to prove that she could fly as well as any man. Her parents lent her the money to buy an airplane.

Amy started on May 5, 1930. Her flight took her over Vienna, Istanbul, and Baghdad. In a sandstorm, she had to make an emergency landing in the desert. Six days later, she arrived in India, beating the record by two days. In Burma she landed on a football field in bad weather. She finally reached Australia. The propeller broke during her last landing, and she had to crash-land.

1. Why didn't Amy have much in common with other girls in her school?
2. Why wasn't she a very successful typist?
3. Who lent her the money to buy a plane?
4. Why did she have to land in the desert?
5. Why did she land in a football field?
6. How did she land in Australia?

Mixed Bag

1. Interview a friend about a "dream job." Take notes, and then write a paragraph.

   1. What kind of job do you want?
   2. When do you want to start work in the morning?
   3. How many coffee breaks do you want?
   4. What time do you want to have lunch?
   5. How much time do you want for lunch?
   6. What time do you want to leave in the afternoon?
   7. What kind of boss do you want? Why?
   8. How much money do you want to make?
   9. Do you want a secretary or an assistant?
   10. Do you want to travel in your job? Where?
   11. Do you want to live close to your job? Why?
   12. How much vacation do you want?

2. Write about the first job you ever had. If you haven't had a job, interview a friend. What kind of job did s(he) have? Did s(he) like it? Why or why not?

3. Interview your father or mother about their jobs. Find out what they like and don't like about their jobs. What kind of "dream job" does your father want? Your mother?

I Think I Could Turn and Live with Animals

I think I could turn and live with animals, they are so
  placid and self-contained,
I stand and look at them long and long,
They do not sweat and whine about their condition,
They do not lie awake in the dark and weep for their
  sins,
They do not make me sick discussing their duty to God,
Not one is dissatisfied, not one is demented with the
  mania of owning things,
Not one kneels to another, nor to his kind that lived
  thousands of years ago,
Not one is respectable or unhappy over the whole earth.

Walt Whitman from *Song of Myself*

Picture This!

Who?   What?   Where?   When?   Why?

Use your imagination as you talk about the photo. Then write about the picture on your own.

Fast Track: *Read and Find Out*

Think about these questions as you read the article.

1. The Olympic Games began as a festival to honor _____.
2. True or false:
   They were intended as more than just sporting contests.
3. In 1896 Baron Pierre de Coubertin revived the idea of the Olympic Games. Find out what you can about these modern-day Games. How are they similar to the original Games? How are they different?

The first Olympic Games were not just sporting contests. There were plays and recitals by poets, as well as races. To the Greeks, the Games expressed the union of mind and body, striving for victory to honor Zeus, the king of the gods.

The events lasted for three days. Athletes ran, wrestled, rode horses and drove chariots. The Games began with the Olympic oath and ended with prizes and feasting.

The Olympic Games continued until 393 AD. They were then forgotten until 1896, when they were revived at Athens on the suggestion of a Frenchman, Baron Pierre de Coubertin. They continue to be held every four years.

WHERE WERE THE FIRST OLYMPIC GAMES HELD?

Every four years, from 776 BC, the Greeks held a great festival. Artists, writers and athletes gathered to honor the great god Zeus. The contests were held at Olympia, and became known as the Olympic Games.

Think about these questions as you read the article.

1. How long does it take for the Earth to travel around the sun?
2. What season is it in Japan when the northern hemisphere is tilted toward the sun?
3. When the sun is overhead at the Tropic of Cancer, what season is it in Argentina?

WHY DO WE HAVE SEASONS?

In one year the Earth travels right around the sun. The diagram shows the Earth at four different times of the year. Notice how the axis remains tilted at the same angle. First one hemisphere, then the other, is tilted towards the sun.

In June, when the northern hemisphere is tilted toward the sun, it is summer in Europe, Asia and North America. The sun is overhead at the Tropic of Cancer. It is then winter in the southern hemisphere.

Six months later, in December, the southern hemisphere is tilted toward the sun. So it is summer at Christmas-time in Australia, but it is winter in Europe.

The sun is overhead at the Tropic of Capricorn. In March and September the sun is overhead at the equator. Both hemispheres are enjoying either autumn or spring.

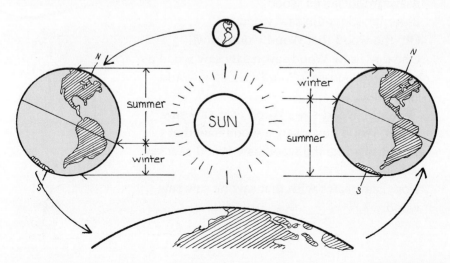

Pronunciation

I.

useful	continue	menu	graduate
usually	cruise	interview	true
humor	huge	beautiful	computer

II.

check	chin	shout	ship
children	chimp	shop	shave
cheap	change	shark	shut

III. *Try these tongue-twisters just for fun!*

A skunk sat on a stump.
The stump thunk the skunk stunk.
The skunk thunk the stump stunk.

Esaw Wood sawed wood.
Esaw Wood would saw wood.
Oh, the wood that Wood would saw!
One day Esaw Wood saw a saw saw wood as
no other wood-saw Wood ever saw would
saw wood.
Of all the wood-saws Wood ever saw saw
wood, Wood never saw a wood-saw that
would saw like the wood-saw Wood saw saw
would.
Now Esaw saws with that saw he saw saw
wood.

Index